AAT

Bookkeeping Transactions

Pocket Notes

These Pocket Notes support study for the following AAT qualifications:

AAT Foundation Certificate in Accounting – Level 2

AAT Foundation Diploma in Accounting and Business – Level 2

AAT Foundation Certificate in Bookkeeping – Level 2

AAT Foundation Award in Accounting Software – Level 2

AAT Level 2 Award in Accounting Skills to Run Your Business

AAT Foundation Certificate in Accounting at SCQF Level 5

British library cataloguing-in-publication data

A catalogue record for this book is available from the British Library.

Published by:
Kaplan Publishing UK
Unit 2 The Business Centre
Molly Millars Lane
Wokingham
Berkshire
RG41 2QZ

ISBN 978-1-78740-813-5

© Kaplan Financial Limited, 2020

Printed and bound in Great Britain.

CONTENTS

Preface

These Pocket Notes contain the key things that you need to know for the exam, presented in a unique visual way that makes revision easy and effective.

Written by experienced lecturers and authors, these Pocket Notes break down content into manageable chunks to maximise your concentration.

Quality and accuracy are of the utmost importance to us so if you spot an error in any of our products, please send an email to mykaplanreporting@kaplan.com with full details, or follow the link to the feedback form in MyKaplan.

Our Quality Co-ordinator will work with our technical team to verify the error and take action to ensure it is corrected in future editions.

A guide to the assessment

The assessment

Bookkeeping Transactions (BTRN) is one of two financial accounting units studied on the Foundation Certificate in Accounting qualification.

Examination

BTRN is assessed by means of a computer based assessment. The CBA will last for 1 hour 30 minutes and consists of 10 tasks.

In any one assessment, students may not be assessed on all content, or on the full depth or breadth of a piece of content. The content assessed may change over time to ensure validity of assessment, but all assessment criteria will be tested over time.

Learning outcomes & weighting

1.	Understand financial transactions within a bookkeeping system	10%
2.	Process customer transactions	10%
3.	Process supplier transactions	15%
4.	Process receipts and payments	25%
5.	Process transactions through the ledgers to the trial balance	40%
	Total	100%

Pass mark

To pass a unit assessment, students need to achieve a mark of 70% or more.

This unit contributes 22% of the total amount required for the Foundation Certificate in Accounting qualification.

1

Business documents

- Business documents for a credit transaction.
- Preparing a sales invoice.
- Types of discounts.
- Preparing credit notes.
- Coding.
- Ordering goods and services.
- Receiving goods.

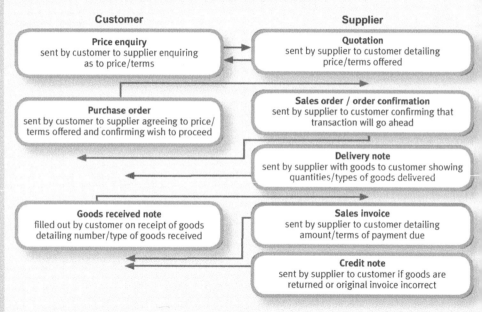

Business documents for a credit transaction

Customer	Supplier

Price enquiry
sent by customer to supplier enquiring as to price/terms

Quotation
sent by supplier to customer detailing price/terms offered

Purchase order
sent by customer to supplier agreeing to price/terms offered and confirming wish to proceed

Sales order / order confirmation
sent by supplier to customer confirming that transaction will go ahead

Delivery note
sent by supplier with goods to customer showing quantities/types of goods delivered

Goods received note
filled out by customer on receipt of goods detailing number/type of goods received

Sales invoice
sent by supplier to customer detailing amount/terms of payment due

Credit note
sent by supplier to customer if goods are returned or original invoice incorrect

Preparing a sales invoice

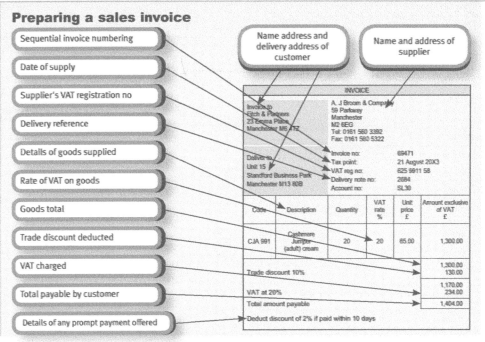

What information is required?

Sales order/ delivery note
(quantity)

Price list
(unit price)

Sales invoice

Customer file
(address etc, discount details)

Types of discounts

Trade discount
% **deducted** from list price for certain valued customers – shown on face of invoice.

Bulk discount
% **deducted** from list price for certain quantity purchased – shown on face of invoice.

Prompt payment discount
% **offered** to certain customers for payment within a certain time period – shown at bottom of invoice.

 CBA focus

The assessment requires you to be able to differentiate between the types of discount.

Preparing credit notes

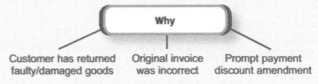

What is a credit note

Issued by supplier to customer to cancel all or part of an invoice

Why

| Customer has returned faulty/damaged goods | Original invoice was incorrect | Prompt payment discount amendment |

What information is required?

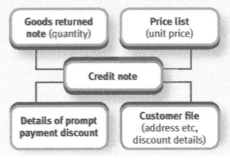

Goods returned note (quantity)

Price list (unit price)

Credit note

Details of prompt payment discount

Customer file (address etc, discount details)

Coding

- relevant to most business documents not just sales invoices/credit notes
- quick, simple method of analysing information for further processing.

Coding and sales invoices/credit notes

- code required for product/type of sale
- customer account code for posting to sales ledger.

Types of codes

Ledger code is a unique reference given to different types of income, expenses, assets and liabilities. It may also be referred to as a general ledger (GL) or nominal code.

Customer account code is a unique reference given to each individual customer of an organisation.

Supplier account code is a unique reference given to each individual supplier of an organisation.

Product code is a unique reference given to each type of product of an organisation.

Coding systems

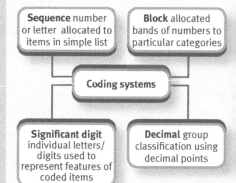

Sequence number or letter allocated to items in simple list

Block allocated bands of numbers to particular categories

Coding systems

Significant digit individual letters/ digits used to represent features of coded items

Decimal group classification using decimal points

Ordering goods and services

Purchase requisition
- internal request to purchasing department for goods/ services
- authorised by department manager

$\downarrow$

Price enquiries
- purchasing department wants to find best price and terms from suppliers

$\downarrow$

Purchase quotations received
- purchasing department can now compare prices and terms and choose best supplier

$\downarrow$

Purchase order
- sent out to chosen supplier

$\downarrow$

Purchase order confirmation
- received from supplier confirming price, discounts delivery details

Purchase order

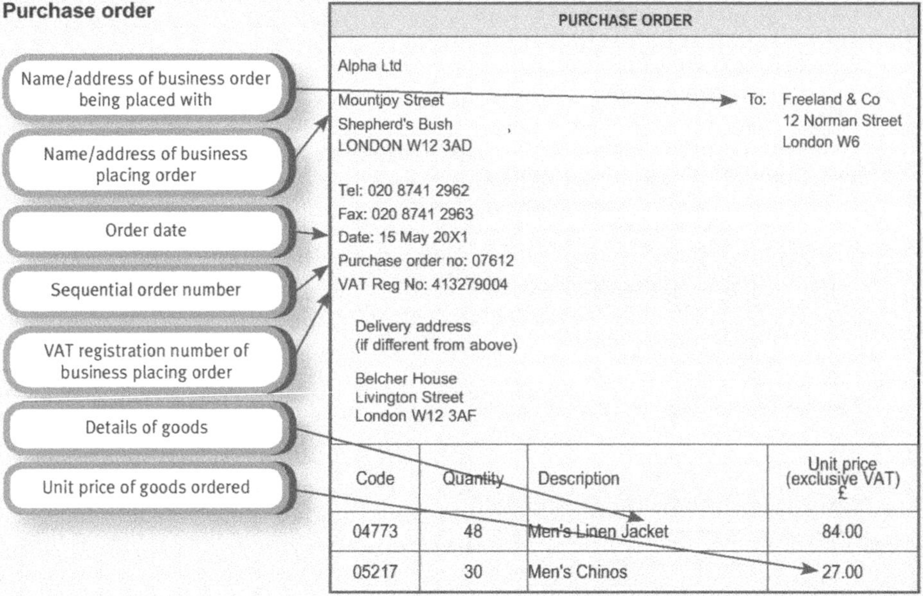
Name/address of business order being placed with
Name/address of business placing order
Order date
Sequential order number
VAT registration number of business placing order
Details of goods
Unit price of goods ordered

PURCHASE ORDER

Alpha Ltd

Mountjoy Street
Shepherd's Bush
LONDON W12 3AD

To: Freeland & Co
12 Norman Street
London W6

Tel: 020 8741 2962
Fax: 020 8741 2963
Date: 15 May 20X1
Purchase order no: 07612
VAT Reg No: 413279004

Delivery address
(if different from above)

Belcher House
Livington Street
London W12 3AF

Code	Quantity	Description	Unit price (exclusive VAT) £
04773	48	Men's Linen Jacket	84.00
05217	30	Men's Chinos	27.00

By telephone
if order placed by telephone details must be confirmed in writing

In writing

Ordering systems

By fax
- similar to in writing but quicker
- order confirmation required

Internet
- only used if allowed business policy
- copy of order must be printed and filed

Receiving goods

Delivery note

- accompanies goods from supplier
- details on delivery note must be checked to actual goods.

DELIVERY NOTE

Deliver to:
Fitch & Partners
Unit 15
Standford Business Park
Manchester
M13 8PB

A. J. Broom & Company Limited
Mountjoy Street
Shepherd's Bush
LONDON W12 3AD
Tel: 0161 560 3392
Fax: 0161 560 5322
Delivery note no: DN4A8372
Date: 25 August 20X3
VAT Reg No: 625 9911 58

Code	Description	Quantity
CJA991	Cashmere Jumper (adult) cream	50

Goods received in good condition

Print name P HARVEY

Signature P Harvey

Date 28/8/X3

Callouts:
- Delivery address
- Name/address of supplier
- Sequential delivery note number
- Date of delivery
- VAT registration number of supplier
- Details/quantity of goods
- Name and signature of person at purchaser's who checks and counts goods

Goods received note
- delivery note is checked as soon as goods arrive
- sometimes a further internal document is filled out once goods have been fully checked
- this is the goods received note
- this details number of goods received and also condition of goods – if some damaged this will be noted
- filed with delivery note.

Debit note and credit note
- if goods received are damaged or not what was ordered they will be returned to supplier
- purchaser may complete a debit note or returns note to accompany returned goods and explain reason for return
- credit note should be received from supplier.

Books of prime entry

- Introduction.
- Sales day book.
- Sales returns day book.
- Purchases day book.
- Purchases returns day book.
- Cash receipts book.
- VAT.
- Cash payments book.
- Discounts allowed book.
- Discounts received book.
- Petty cash book.

Introduction

Rather than entering each individual transaction into the ledger accounts as they happen, books of prime entry are used to record transactions/documents of the same type before they are processed further.

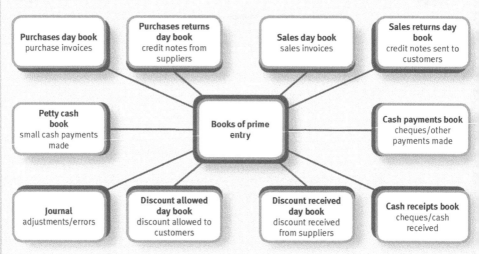

Sales day book

- list of invoices sent out to credit customers
- date
- invoice number
- customer name/account code
- invoice total analysed into net, VAT and gross (total)

- information copied from sales invoices
- before further processing must be totalled
- totals can be checked by cross casting £3,794.14 + £758.82 = £4,552.96.

Sales Day book						
Date	Invoice No	Customer Name	Sales ledger code	Total (gross) £	VAT (20%) £	Net £
12/08/X3	69489	TJ Builder	SL21	2,004.12	334.02	1,670.10
12/08/X3	69490	McCarthy & Sons	SL08	1,485.74	247.62	1,238.12
12/08/X3	69491	Trevor Partner	SL10	1,063.10	177.18	885.92
				4,552.96	758.82	3,794.14

Analysed sales day book

Sometimes the net figure (actual sales) is analysed into different types of sale/product type.

| Sales day book | | | | | | | | | | |
Date	Invoice No	Customer Name	Code	Total (gross) £	VAT £	Russia £	Poland £	Spain £	Germany £	France £
15/08/X1	167	Worldwide News	W5	3,000.00	500.00					2,500.00
	168	Local News	L1	240.00	40.00			200.00		
	169	The Press Today	P2	360.00	60.00				300.00	
	170	Home Call	H1	240.00	40.00			200.00		
	171	Tomorrow	T1	120.00	20.00					100.00
	172	Worldwide news	W5	3,600.00	600.00	3,000.00	–			
				7,560.00	1,260.00	3,000.00	–	400.00	300.00	2,600.00

Sales returns day book

- list of credit notes sent out to credit customers
- date
- credit note number
- customer name/account code
- credit note total analysed into net, VAT and total
- information copied from credit note.

SALES RETURNS DAY BOOK						
Date	Credit Note No.	Customer Name	Code	Total (gross) £	VAT £	Net £
28/08/X3	03561	Trevor Partner	SL10	125.48	20.91	104.57
28/08/X3	03562	TJ Builder	SL21	151.74	25.29	126.45
				277.22	46.20	231.02

Purchases day book

- list of invoices received from credit suppliers
- date
- purchase invoice number (often internal consecutive number allocated)
- supplier name/account code

- invoice total analysed into net, VAT and total (gross)
- information copied from purchase invoice
- before further processing must be totalled
- totals can be checked by cross casting £663.90 + £132.77 = £796.67.

PURCHASES DAY BOOK						
Date	Invoice No.	code	supplier	Total (gross) £	VAT £	Net £
20X1						
7 May	2814	PL06	J Taylor	190.41	31.73	158.68
8 May	2815	PL13	McMinn Partners	288.14	48.02	240.12
	2816	PL27	D B Bros	96.54	16.09	80.45
9 May	2817	PL03	J S Ltd	221.58	36.93	184.65
				796.67	132.77	663.90

Analysed purchases day book

Sometimes the net figure (actual purchases)
is analysed into different types of purchase/
product type.

PURCHASES DAY BOOK									
Date	Invoice no	Code	Supplier	Total (gross) £	VAT £	01 £	02 £	03 £	04 £
05/02/X5	1161	053	Calderwood & Co	20.16	3.36	16.80			
05/02/X5	1162	259	Mellor & Cross	112.86	18.81		94.05		
05/02/X5	1163	360	Thompson Bros Ltd	42.86	7.14	35.72			

Purchases returns day book

- list of credit notes received from credit suppliers
- date
- credit note number (often internal consecutive number allocated)
- customer name/account code
- credit note total analysed into net, VAT and total
- information copied from credit note.

PURCHASES RETURNS DAY BOOK						
Date	Credit note no	Supplier	Code	Total (gross) £	VAT £	Net £
09/05/X1	02456	McMinn Partners	PL13	64.80	10.80	54.00
09/05/X1	02457	J S Ltd	PL03	72.00	12.00	60.00
				136.80	22.80	114.00

Cash receipts book

The cash receipts book records all money received into the business bank account for whatever reason.

Cash receipts book						
Date	Narrative	Total £	VAT £	Receivables £	Cash sales £	Sundry £
3 Jul	A Brown	20.54	3.42		17.12	
5 Jul	S Smith & Co Ltd	9.30		9.30		
	P Priest	60.80		60.80		
	James & Jeans	39.02	6.50		32.52	
	LS Moore	17.00		17.00		
6 Jul	L White Ltd	5.16		5.16		
7 Jul	M N Furnishers Ltd	112.58				112.58
	R B Roberts	23.65		23.65		
	Light and Shade	86.95		86.95		
		375.00	9.92	202.86	49.64	112.58

- Date of receipt
- Details of receipt
- Total of receipts
- Total VAT on cash sales
- Total receipts from receivables
- Total receipt for cash sales
- Total receipts from sundry income

- entries to the cash receipts book come from either the remittance list or a photocopy of the paying in slip
- to check the totalling the cross casts should be checked:

	£
VAT	9.92
Receivables	202.86
Cash sales	49.64
Sundry income	112.58
Total	375.00

VAT

- VAT is only ever recorded in the cash receipts book on cash sales or other income
- any VAT on sales on credit (i.e. receipts from receivables) has already been recorded in the sales day book and posted to the ledger accounts from there.

Cash payments book

The cash payments book records all money paid out of the business bank account for whatever reason.

Date	Details	Cheque No	Total	VAT	Purchases ledger £	Cash	Post
14/2	K Ellis	1152	80.00		80.00		
15/2	Hutt Ltd	1153	120.00	20.00		100.00	
16/2	Biggs Ltd	1154	200.00				200.00
			400.00	20.00	80.00	100.00	200.00

| Date of payment | Details of payment | Total of payment | Total VAT on cash purchases | Total payment to payables | Total payment for cash purchases | Total payment for post |

- entries to the cash payments book come from either the cheque stubs or other banking documentation (see later chapter)
- to check the totalling the cross casts should be checked:

	£
VAT	20.00
Purchases ledger	80.00
Cash purchases	100.00
Post	200.00
Total	400.00

VAT is only ever recorded in the cash payments book on cash purchases or other payments for expenditure that attracts VAT that have not been entered in the purchases day book.

- any VAT on purchases on credit (i.e. payments to payables) has already been recorded in the purchases day book and posted to the ledger accounts from there.

KAPLAN PUBLISHING

Discounts allowed book

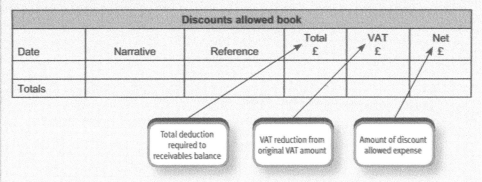

Discounts allowed book					
Date	Narrative	Reference	Total £	VAT £	Net £
Totals					

Total deduction required to receivables balance

VAT reduction from original VAT amount

Amount of discount allowed expense

The discount allowed day book records the credit notes issued due to a customer taking advantage of a prompt payment discount.

Discounts received book

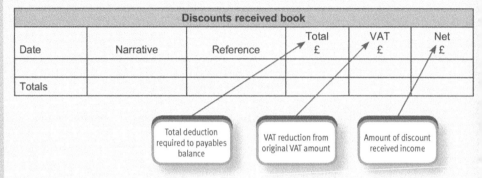

Discounts received book					
Date	Narrative	Reference	Total £	VAT £	Net £
Totals					

Total deduction required to payables balance

VAT reduction from original VAT amount

Amount of discount received income

The discounts received day book records the credit notes received from a supplier due to us taking advantage of a prompt payment discount.

Petty cash book

- book of prime entry
- often part of general ledger as well
- small cash receipts side
- larger analysed cash payments side.

Receipts side – only one column as only entry is regular payment in cash from bank

Payments side – analysed according to typical expenditure plus VAT column

PETTY CASH BOOK

RECEIPTS ◄   **PAYMENTS** ◄

Date	Narrative	Total £	Date	Narrative	Voucher no	Total £	Postage £	Cleaning £	Tea & Coffee £	Sundry £	VAT £
1 Nov	Bal b/f	35.50									
1 Nov	Cheque	114.50	1 Nov	ASDA	58	23.50			23.50		
			2 Nov	Post Office Ltd	59	29.50	29.50				
			2 Nov	Cleaning materials	60	15.07		12.56			2.51
			3 Nov	Postage	61	16.19	16.19				
			3 Nov	ASDA	62	10.57		8.81			1.76
			4 Nov	Newspapers	63	18.90				18.90	
			5 Nov	ASDA	64	12.10				10.09	2.01
						125.83	45.69	21.37	23.50	28.99	6.28

Imprest amount of £150 to start week

Date of claim

Details

Sequential petty cash voucher number

Analysed payments – total column includes VAT but analysis column amount is net of VAT

When petty cash book has been written up for a period it must be totalled. Totals should then be checked by cross-casting:

	£
Postage	45.69
Cleaning	21.37
Tea & coffee	23.50
Sundry	28.99
VAT	6.28
Total	125.83

3

Double entry bookkeeping
– an introduction

- Principles of double entry bookkeeping.
- The accounting equation.
- Types of income and expense.

Principles of double entry bookkeeping

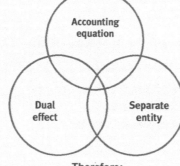

- each transaction has two financial effects

Accounting equation

Dual effect

Separate entity

- the owner of the business is a separate entity from the business.

Therefore:

- each transaction has both a debit and a credit entry in the ledger accounts.

- the amount invested into the business by the owner is kept separate, it is known as "capital". The amount withdrawn from the business by the owner for their own personal use, it is known as "drawings".
- Note: capital and drawings are not necessarily just cash, an owner can invest and withdraw other assets.

Accounting equation

Assets – Liabilities = Capital

Terminology

Asset
- something owned by the business

Liability
- something owed by the business

Capital
- amount the owner has invested in the business

Receivable
- someone who owes the business money

Payable
- someone the business owes money to

The accounting equation

Example

Accounting equation

(i) Ted pays £10,000 into a business bank account to start a business.

Dual effect	**Assets (cash)**	**Capital**
	£10,000	= £10,000

(ii) Ted buys goods to resell for £3,000 in cash

Dual effect	Assets (cash) + assets (inventory)	Capital
	£7,000 + £3,000	= £10,000

(iii) Ted sells the goods for cash for £4,000.

These goods were bought for £3,000, which is £1,000 less than what they have now been sold for. Therefore, a profit of £1,000 has been made.

This is added to the capital balance as it is an increase in the amount owed back to the owner of the business.

Dual effect	Assets (cash)	Capital	Profit
	£11,000	= £10,000	+ £1,000

(iv) Ted purchases more goods for £6,000 on credit

Dual effect	Assets (inventory)	Liabilities (payable)	Capital + Profit
	£11,000 + £6,000	– £6,000	= £11,000

(v) Ted sells these goods for £8,000 on credit

Dual effect	Assets – Liabilities (receivables)	Capital + Profit
	£11,000 + £8,000 – £6,000	= £11,000 + £2,000

(vi) Ted pays £500 of rent for his premises. This reduces his cash and profit by £500

Dual effect	Assets (cash)	Capital + Profit
	£10,500 + £8,000 – £6,000	= £11,000 + £1,500

Types of income and expense

Capital income

Income received from the sale of non-current assets

Example: The proceeds received from selling a motor vehicle

Revenue income

Income received from the trading activities

Example: The proceeds received from selling goods (inventory)

Capital expenditure

Expense of acquiring or improving non-current assets

Examples: Buying a piece of machinery, removing single glazed windows and replacing with double glazed windows

Revenue expenditure

Day to day running expenses of the business, including the repair and maintenance of non-current assets.

Examples: Gas, electricity, rent, repairs and maintenance

4

Ledger accounting

- Ledger accounts.
- General rules of double entry bookkeeping.
- Accounting for cash transactions.
- Accounting for credit transactions.
- Balancing the ledger accounts.
- What is a trial balance?

Ledger accounts

Typical ledger account:

Title of account

Date Narrative	£	Date Narrative	£
DEBIT side		CREDIT side	

The dual effect means that every transaction has a debit entry in one account and a credit entry in another account.

Key question – which account is the debit entry to and which account is the credit entry to?

Definition

A **cash transaction** means a transaction which is paid for immediately.

Definition

A **credit transaction** is a transaction that is only paid after an agreed period of time, e.g. 30 days.

Note that the terms 'cash', 'cheque' are used interchangeably in the early part of your studies. If the person pays by cash or cheque, the money will be entered into the 'bank' account (sometimes called the 'cash account').

Thus if John buys a car for £4,000 and pays immediately with a cheque or cash, that is a cash transaction.

If John buys a car for £4,000 on credit, when he eventually pays he can pay with either cash or a cheque – it makes no difference – it will be a credit transaction.

General rules of double entry bookkeeping

The table below summarises the effect a debit (DR) or a credit (CR) entry can have.

Ledger account

DEBIT	£	CREDIT	£
Money in		Money out	
Increase in asset		Increase in liability	
Decrease in liability		Decrease in asset	
Increase in expense		Increase in income	

The mnemonic **DEAD CLIC** is a great way to remember the side to post a debit or credit entry to.

DRs increase;	CRs increase;
Expenses	Liabilities
Assets	Income
Drawings	Capital

Accounting for cash transactions

Example

Cash transactions

(i) Payment of £10,000 into business bank account by owner:

Debit   Bank (money in)

Credit Capital (increase in liability – amount owed to owner)

Bank account				Capital account			
	£		£		£		£
Capital	10,000					Bank	10,000

(ii) Purchase of goods for cash of £3,000

Debit   Purchases (expense)

Credit Bank (money out)

Purchases account				Bank account			
	£		£		£		£
Bank	3,000					Purchases	3,000

(iii) Sale of goods for cash of £4,000
    Debit Bank (money in)
    Credit Sales (income)

Bank account				Sales account			
	£		£		£		£
Sales	4,000					Bank	4,000

(iv) Payment of rent in cash £500
    Debit   Rent (expense)
    Credit Bank (money out)

Rent account				Bank account			
	£		£		£		£
Bank	500					Rent	500

Accounting for credit transactions

(i) Purchases goods for £6,000 on credit
    Debit   Purchases (expense)
    Credit Payables (liability)

Purchases account		
	£	£
Payables	6,000	

Payables account		
	£	£
	Purchases	6,000

(ii) Sale of goods on credit for £8,000
    Debit   Receivables (asset)
    Credit Sales (income)

Receivables account		
	£	£
Sales	8,000	

Sales account		
	£	£
	Receivables	8,000

(iii) Payment of part of money owed to credit supplier of £1,500

Debit   Payables (reduction in liability)
Credit Bank (money out)

Payables account			
	£		£
Bank	1,500		

Bank account			
	£		£
		Payables	1,500

(iv) Receipt of part of money owed by credit customer of £5,000

Debit   Bank (money in)
Credit Receivables (reduction in asset)

Bank account			
	£		£
Receivables	5,000		

Receivables account			
	£		£
		Bank	5,000

Balancing the ledger accounts

At various points in time the owner/owners of a business will need information about the total transactions in the period. E.g. total sales, amount of payables outstanding, amount of cash remaining. This can be found by balancing the ledger accounts.

Example

Here is a typical cash (or bank) account:

Cash account

	£		£
Capital	10,000	Purchases	3,000
Sales	4,000	Rent	500
Receivables	5,000	Payables	1,500

Step 1 Total both the debit side and the credit side and make a note of the totals.

Step 2 The higher of the totals should be inserted at the bottom of both the debit side and the credit side (leaving a line before inserting the totals).

Cash account

	£		£
Capital	10,000	Purchases	3,000
Sales	4,000	Rent	500
Receivables	5,000	Payables	1,500
	19,000		19,000

Step 3 On the side that amounts to the lower total, insert the figure that makes that side add up to the higher total. This balance should have the narrative "balance carried down" ("balance c/d").

Cash account

	£		£
Capital	10,000	Purchases	3,000
Sales	4,000	Rent	500
Receivables	5,000	Payables	1,500
		Balance c/d	14,000
	19,000		19,000

Step 4 On the opposite side to where the "balance carried down" has been inserted, enter the same figure below the total line. This should be referred to as "balance brought down" ("balance b/d").

Cash account

	£		£
Capital	10,000	Purchases	3,000
Sales	4,000	Rent	500
Receivables	5,000	Payables	1,500
		Balance c/d	14,000
	19,000		19,000
Balance b/d	14,000		

This shows that after all of these transactions there is £14,000 of cash left as an asset in the business (a debit balance brought down = an asset).

CBA focus

In the assessment you will be required to balance a number of ledger accounts and you must be able to select the correct narratives to be used when balancing an account off.

What is a trial balance?

- list of all of the ledger balances in the general ledger
- debit balances and credit balances listed separately
- debit balance total should equal credit balance total.

Example

Trial balance

	Debit balances £	Credit balances £
Sales		5,000
Wages	100	
Purchases	3,000	
Rent	200	
Car	3,000	
Receivables	100	
Payables		1,400
	6,400	6,400

Debit or credit balance?

If you are just given a list of balances you must know whether they are debit or credit balances.

Remember the rules!

In the assessment you will either have to enter a number of balances in the trial balance from ledger accounts that have been balanced or you will be given a list of balances that you then have to determine which side of the trial balance they should appear on.

Debit balances	Credit balances
Expense	Liability
Asset	Income
Drawings	Capital

5

Accounting for credit sales, VAT and discounts

- Accounting for credit sales.
- VAT and discounts.
- Accounting for credit sales returns.

Accounting for credit sales

The double entry for a sale including VAT:

Dr	Receivables	X	(gross – VAT inclusive)
Cr	VAT (sales tax)	X	(VAT)
Cr	Sales	X	(net – VAT exclusive)

VAT and discounts

A trade discount or a bulk discount is a definite reduction to the list price of a product or service. These discounts will be deducted prior to VAT being calculated.

A prompt payment discount is merely offered to the customer on the invoice. No deduction to the invoice value or to the VAT calculation takes place until the customer takes advantage of this discount by making a payment within the required time.

Example

Goods are despatched to a customer with a list price of £1,000. The customer is allowed a trade discount of 20% and is offered a prompt payment discount of 4% if the invoice is paid within 10 days.

Invoice amounts:	
	£
List price	1,000.00
Less: trade discount	(200.00)
	800.00
VAT (see below)	160.00
Invoice total	960.00
VAT calculation	£800 x 20%

NB The VAT has been calculated based on £800 (list price less trade discount).

Accounting for credit sales returns

The double entry for a sales return including VAT (sales tax) is:

Dr	Sales returns	X	(net – VAT exclusive)
Dr	VAT (sales tax)	X	(VAT)
Cr	Receivables	X	(gross – VAT inclusive)

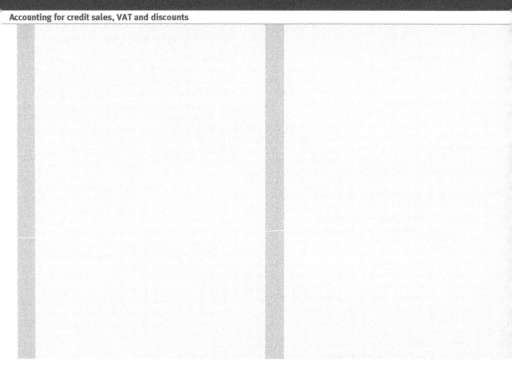

6

Accounting for credit purchases, VAT and discounts

- Accounting for credit purchases.
- VAT and discounts.
- Accounting for credit purchases returns.

Accounting for credit purchases

The double entry for a purchase including VAT:

Dr	Purchases	X	(net – VAT exclusive)
Dr	VAT (sales tax)	X	(VAT)
Cr	Payables	X	(gross – VAT inclusive)

VAT and discounts

VAT and discounts have already been studied when considering sales in chapter 5. The calculations of VAT and discounts are exactly the same when considering purchases.

The purchaser receives a "sales invoice" from the seller but the purchaser refers to this as a "purchase invoice" and enters it into the books accordingly. It is the same document but is referred to differently by the different parties involved in the transaction.

Ensure that you are happy with the calculations of VAT and discounts by reviewing over these in chapter 5.

Accounting for credit purchases returns

The double entry for a purchases return including VAT (sales tax) is:

Dr	Payables	X	(gross – VAT inclusive)
Cr	VAT (sales tax)	X	(VAT)
Cr	Purchases returns	X	(net – VAT exclusive)

7

Control accounts and subsidiary ledgers

- Introduction.
- Sales ledger control account.
- Posting the sales day book.
- Posting the sales returns day book.
- Purchases ledger control account.
- Posting the purchases day book.
- Posting the purchases returns day book.

Introduction

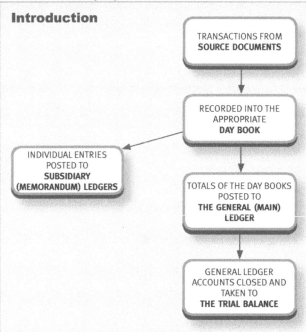

TRANSACTIONS FROM
SOURCE DOCUMENTS

RECORDED INTO THE
APPROPRIATE
DAY BOOK

INDIVIDUAL ENTRIES
POSTED TO
**SUBSIDIARY
(MEMORANDUM) LEDGERS**

TOTALS OF THE DAY BOOKS
POSTED TO
**THE GENERAL (MAIN)
LEDGER**

GENERAL LEDGER
ACCOUNTS CLOSED AND
TAKEN TO
THE TRIAL BALANCE

Sales ledger control account

- total receivables account
- sales invoices posted from sales day book
- credit notes posted from sales returns day book
- receipts from customers posted from cash receipts book
- discounts allowed to customers posted from discounts allowed day book.

Posting the sales day book

General ledger

- at the end of each day/week/month SDB is totalled
- totals must then be posted to accounts in the general ledger.

Double entry:

Debit	Sales Ledger Control Account	Total (gross) figure
Credit	Sales account	Net figure
Credit	VAT account	VAT amount

SALES DAY BOOK

Date	Invoice No	Customer Name	Sales ledger code	Total (gross) £	VAT £	Net £
12/08/X3	69489	TJ Builder	SL21	2,004.12	334.02	1,670.10
12/08/X3	69490	McCarthy & Sons	SL08	1,485.74	247.62	1,238.12
12/08/X3	69491	Trevor Partner	SL10	1,063.10	177.18	885.92
				4,552.96	758.82	3,794.14

Debit sales ledger control account

Credit VAT

Credit sales

Sales Ledger Control Account

	£		£
SDB	4,552.96		

Sales account

	£		£
		SDB	3,794.14

VAT

	£		£
		SDB	758.82

Note:

For the purposes of the examples in this chapter, the narratives in the ledger accounts are references to the appropriate day books, showing the source of the data.

Subsidiary (sales) ledger

- SLCA records the amount owing by all of the business's credit customers in total
- but also need information about each individual credit customer's balance
- therefore ledger account kept for each individual customer in a subsidiary ledger, the subsidiary (sales) ledger.

Subsidiary (sales) ledger

Customer A

	£		£

Customer B

	£		£

Customer C

	£		£

Posting to the subsidiary (sales) ledger

- each individual entry from the sales day book must be entered into the relevant customer account in the subsidiary (sales) ledger
- amount entered is the gross invoice total (including VAT)
- entered on the debit side of the account indicating that this is the amount the receivable owes.

Example

Now we return to the sales day book from earlier and post the individual entries to the subsidiary (sales) ledger.

TJ Builder

	£		£
SDB	2,004.12		

McCarthy & Sons

	£		£
SDB	1,485.74		

Trevor Partner

	£		£
SDB	1,063.10		

Posting the sales returns day book

General ledger

- as with the SDB the SRDB must also be posted to the general ledger accounts and subsidiary (sales) ledger accounts.

Double entry:

Debit	Sales returns account	Net figure
Debit	VAT account	VAT total
Credit	Sales Ledger Control Account	Total (gross) figure

SALES RETURNS DAY BOOK

Date	Credit Note No.	Customer Name	Code	Total (gross) £	VAT £	Net £
28/08/X3	03561	Trevor Partner	SL10	125.48	20.91	104.57
28/08/X3	03562	TJ Builder	SL21	151.74	25.29	126.45
				277.22	46.20	231.02

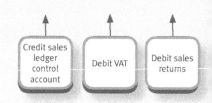

Credit sales ledger control account

Debit VAT

Debit sales returns

Sales Ledger Control Account

	£		£
SDB	4,552.96	SRDB	277.22

Sales account

	£		£
		SDB	3,794.14

VAT account

	£		£
SRDB	46.20	SDB	758.82

Sales returns account

	£		£
SRDB	231.02		

Subsidiary (sales) ledger

Each individual credit note must be entered in the customer's account:

- gross credit note total
- credit individual receivable account (reducing the amount owed).

T J Builder

	£		£
SDB	2,004.12	SRDB	151.74

McCarthy & Sons

	£		£
SDB	1,485.74		

Trevor Partner

	£		£
SDB	1,063.10	SRDB	125.48

In the assessment you will be required to post the sales day book/sales returns day book and the purchases day book/purchases returns day book to the general ledger and the relevant subsidiary ledger.

Purchases ledger control account

- total payables account
- purchase invoices posted from purchases day book
- credit notes posted from purchases returns day book
- payments to suppliers posted from cash payments book
- discounts received from suppliers posted from discounts received day book.

Posting the purchases day book (PDB)

General ledger

- at the end of each day/week/month PDB is totalled
- totals must then be posted to accounts in the general ledger.

Double entry:

Debit	Purchases account	Net figure
Debit	VAT account amount	VAT
Credit	Purchases Ledger Control Account (PLCA)	Total (gross) figure

PURCHASES DAY BOOK						
Date	Invoice No.	Code	Supplier	Total (gross) £	VAT £	Net £
20X1						
7 May	2814	PL06	J Taylor	190.41	31.73	158.68
8 May	2815	PL13	McMinn Partners	288.14	48.02	240.12
	2816	PL27	D B Bros	96.54	16.09	80.45
9 May	2817	PL03	J S Ltd	221.58	36.93	184.65
				796.67	132.77	663.90

Credit purchases ledger control account

Debit VAT

Debit purchases

Purchases account

	£		£
PDB	663.90		

VAT account

	£		£
PDB	132.77		

Purchases ledger control account

	£		£
		PDB	796.67

Subsidiary purchases ledger

- The PLCA records the amount owing to all of the business's credit suppliers in total
- but also need information about each individual credit supplier's balance
- therefore ledger account kept for each individual supplier in a subsidiary ledger, the subsidiary (purchases) ledger.

Subsidiary (Purchases) Ledger

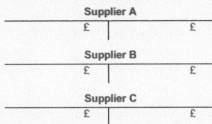

Supplier A

£		£

Supplier B

£		£

Supplier C

£		£

Posting to the subsidiary (purchases) ledger

- each individual entry from the purchases day book must be entered into the relevant supplier account in the subsidiary (purchases) ledger
- amount entered is the gross invoice total (including VAT)
- entered on the credit side of the account indicating that this is the amount owed to the supplier.

Example continued

Now we return to the purchases day book from earlier and post the individual entries to the subsidiary (purchases) ledger.

J Taylor		
£		£
	PDB	190.41

D B Bros		
£		£
	PDB	96.54

McMinn Partners		
£		£
	PDB	288.14

J S Ltd		
£		£
	PDB	221.58

Posting the purchases returns day book (PRDB)

PURCHASES RETURNS DAY BOOK						
Date	Credit note no	Supplier	Code	Total (gross) £	VAT £	Net £
09/05/X1	02456	McMinn Partners	PL13	64.80	10.80	54.00
09/05/X1	02457	J S Ltd	PL03	72.00	12.00	60.00
				136.80	22.80	114.00

Debit purchases ledger control account

Credit VAT

Credit purchases returns

General ledger

- as with the PDB the PRDB must also be posted to the general ledger accounts and subsidiary (purchases) ledger accounts.

Double entry:

Debit	Purchases Ledger Control Account	Total (gross) figure
Credit	Purchases returns account	Net figure
Credit	VAT account total	VAT

Purchases account

	£		£
PDB	663.90		

VAT account

	£		£
PDB	132.77	PRDB	22.80

Purchase Ledger Control Account

	£		£
PRDB	136.80	PDB	796.67

Purchases returns account

	£		£
		PRDB	114.00

Subsidiary (purchases) ledger

Each individual credit note must be entered in the supplier's account:

* gross credit note total

debit individual supplier account (reducing the amount owing).

CBA focus

In the assessment you will be required to post the sales day book/sales returns day and the purchases day book/purchases returns day book to the general ledger and the relevant subsidiary ledger.

J Taylor

	£		£
		PDB	190.41

McMinn Partners

	£		£
PRDB	64.80	PDB	288.14

D B Bros

	£		£
		PDB	96.54

J S Ltd

	£		£
PRDB	72.00	PDB	221.58

8

Receipts and payments

- Posting
  - cash receipts book and the discounts allowed book to the general ledger.
  - discounts allowed day book.
  - cash receipts book and discounts allowed book to the subsidiary ledger.
- Checks to make on purchase invoices.
- Posting
  - cash payments book and discounts received book to the general ledger.
  - discounts received day book.
  - cash payments book and discounts received book to subsidiary ledger.
- Petty cash
  - system
  - vouchers
  - book
  - posting
  - reconciling
  - control account
  - control account reconciliation.

Receivables' statements

- sent by supplier to customer usually monthly
- reminder of amounts due.

STATEMENT OF ACCOUNT				
Invoice to Fitch & Partners 23 Emma Place Manchester M6 4TZ		NICK BROOKS 225 School Lane Weymouth, Dorset WE36 5NR Tel: 0149 29381 Fax: 0149 29382 Date: 30/04/X2		
Date	Transaction	Debit £	Credit £	Balance £
03/04	INV001	185.65		185.65
10/04	CN001		49.35	136.30
14/04	INV005	206.80		343.10
18/04	PAYMENT		136.30	206.80
21/04	INV007	253.80		460.60
26/04	INV008	192.70		653.30
May we remind you that our credit terms are 30 days With 3% discount for payment within 14 days				

Aged debt analysis

- internal document
- prepared for each individual customer
- shows the age of amounts outstanding
- useful for identifying slow paying/problem customers.

Customer	Total £	<30 days £	30 to 60 days £	>60 days £
H Hardy	689.46	368.46	321.00	–
L Framer	442.79	379.60	–	63.19
K Knight	317.68	–	169.46	148.22

Posting the cash receipts book and the discounts allowed book to the general ledger

Basic double entry for cash receipts:

Debit	Bank account
Credit	Sales Ledger Control Account (receipts from receivables)
	Sales (cash sales)
	Other income (e.g. rent)

In most cases the cash receipts book is not only a book of prime entry but also part of the general ledger in which case the debit entry for the total column is not required.

Double entry for discounts allowed:

Debit	Discounts allowed
Debit	VAT
Credit	Sales Ledger Control Account

Postings

Cash receipts book						
Date	Narrative	Total £	VAT £	Receivables £	Cash sales £	Sundry £
3 Jul	A Brown	20.54	3.42		17.12	
5 Jul	S Smith & Co Ltd	9.30		9.30		
	P Priest	60.80		60.80		
	James & Jeans	39.02	6.50		32.52	
	LS Moore	17.00		17.00		
6 Jul	L White Ltd	5.16		5.16		
7 Jul	M N Furnishers Ltd	112.58				112.58
	R B Roberts	23.65		23.65		
	Light and Shade	86.95		86.95		
		375.00	9.92	202.86	49.64	112.58

Credit VAT account

Credit sales ledger control account

Credit sales account

Credit sundry income account

Posting the discounts allowed day book

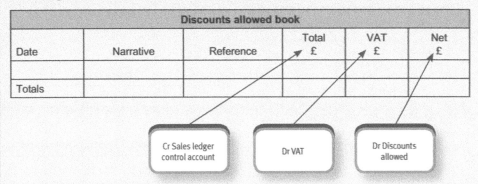

Discounts allowed book					
Date	Narrative	Reference	Total £	VAT £	Net £
Totals					

Cr Sales ledger control account

Dr VAT

Dr Discounts allowed

Posting the cash receipts book and discount allowed book to the subsidiary ledger

- after the totals have been posted to the general ledger from the cash receipts book the individual entries in the receivables column must be posted to the subsidiary (sales) ledger

- each cash receipt is credited to the individual receivable account (reduction of amount owing)

- each discount allowed is credited to the individual receivable account (reduction of amount owing).

Subsidiary sales ledger – postings (extracts)

Smith & Co Ltd

£		£
	CRB	9.30

L S Moore

£		£
	CRB	17.00
	DAB	1.00

The cash receipts from Smith & Co and L S Moore have been taken from the cash receipts book. L S Moore received a prompt payment discount of £1.00 (gross).

Checks to make on purchase invoices

Once a purchase invoice is received from a supplier a number of checks must be made on it to ensure that it is valid before it is authorised for payment.

Purchase order
- details of invoice checked to purchase order to ensure goods were ordered

Trade discounts
- check supplier's file or price quotation to ensure trade discount % correct
- check file/quotation even if no discount is shown
- check calculation

Prompt payment discount
- check supplier's file of price quotation to ensure prompt payment discount % given
- also check if no discount is shown

Checks on purchase invoices

Goods received note/delivery note
- to ensure goods were actually received

Bulk discount
- check supplier's file or price quotation to ensure correct discount for bulk purchase has been given
- check calculation

VAT calculation
- check VAT correctly calculated particularly if prompt payment discount offered (see earlier chapter for calculation).

Invoices for services
- no delivery note but accuracy of invoice must be checked
- invoice details must be checked and authorised by appropriate person

Credit notes

The same checks as above should be made credit notes received from suppliers.

Example of authorisation stamp

Account code is purchase ledger code

Purchase order no	436129
Invoice No	388649
Cheque no	
Account code	PL70
Checked	J Wilmber
Date	03/05/X4
General ledger account	

Cheque number inserted when payment made

Signed when all checks are made on invoice

Once the invoice has been authorised the amount to be paid must be calculated. This may entail the complication of prompt payment discounts, as seen previously.

Example

An invoice is received from a supplier as follows:

	£
List price	1,000.00
Trade discount	(200.00)
	800.00
VAT	160.00
	960.00

A 4% prompt payment discount is offered for payment within 14 days.

If the prompt payment discount is taken - the amount paid will be £960 less 4% which equals £921.60. This is made up of a revised net amount of £768 and a revised VAT charge of £153.60.

Payment by invoice

- each invoice paid at latest date allowed by credit terms
- must ensure that if the business policy is to take cash discounts then invoice is paid in time to reach supplier within agreed period

Payment on set date

- this may be one day per week/month but this may mean that cash discounts are lost
- alternative to set day per week/fortnight when all invoices which will have exceeded credit/settlement discount limit by following payment date are paid

Methods of scheduling of payments

Payment of supplier's statements

- received monthly showing invoices outstanding
- must be checked to supplier's account to ensure correct
- invoices on statement will be paid according to business policy
- often remittance advice attached to statement to show amounts being paid

Posting the cash payments book and the discounts received book to the general ledger

Basic double entry for cash payments :

Debit   Purchases for cash
Debit   Purchases ledger control account
Debit   Other expenses
Credit   Bank account

In most cases the cash payments book is not only a book of prime entry but also part of the general ledger in which case the credit entry for the total column is not required.

Double entry for discounts received:

Debit   Purchases ledger control account
Credit   Discounts received
Credit   VAT

Postings

Cash payments book							
Date	Details	Cheque No	Total	VAT £	Purchase ledger £	Cash purchases £	Post £
14/2	K Ellis	1152	80.00		80.00		
15/2	Hutt Ltd	1153	120.00	20.00		100.00	
16/2	Biggs Ltd	1154	200.00				200.00
			400.00	20.00	80.00	100.00	200.00

Debit VAT account

Debit purchases ledger control account

Debit cash purchases

Debit post

Posting the discounts received day book

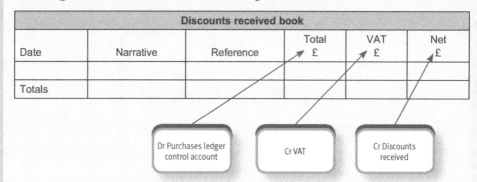

Discounts received book					
Date	Narrative	Reference	Total £	VAT £	Net £
Totals					

Dr Purchases ledger control account

Cr VAT

Cr Discounts received

Posting the cash payments book and discounts received book to the subsidiary ledger

- after the totals have been posted to the general ledger from the cash payments book the individual entries in the purchase ledger column must be posted to the subsidiary (purchases) ledger

- each cash payment is debited to the individual payable account (reduction of amount owing)

- each discount received is debited to the individual payable account (reduction of amount owing).

Subsidiary (purchases) ledger – postings (extracts)

K Ellis

	£		£
CPB	80.00		
DRB	2.00		

K Ellis payment of £80.00 was detailed in the cash payments book. A discount received of £2.00 (gross) was also recorded.

The cash book as part of the general ledger

The two sides of the cash book which are the cash receipts and the cash payments have been reviewed already as separate books.

The assessment often shows the cashbook as a ledger account format. This means that the cashbook actually forms a part of the general ledger, with the entries being one side of the double entry required within the general ledger.

The requirement will be to complete the other side of the entry within the general ledger, and to update the individual accounts in the subsidiary ledger.

Petty cash system

Most businesses require small amounts of cash for small cash expenses and reimbursement of business expenditure incurred by employees.

```
┌─────────────────────────────────────┐
│ Employee incurs expense e.g. purchase │
│         stamps for office             │
└─────────────────────────────────────┘
                  ↓
┌─────────────────────────────────────┐
│ Fills out petty cash voucher for amount │
│         and attaches receipt          │
└─────────────────────────────────────┘
                  ↓
┌─────────────────────────────────────┐
│ Takes to petty cashier who checks voucher │
│   and receipt and authorises voucher  │
└─────────────────────────────────────┘
                  ↓
┌─────────────────────────────────────┐
│ Petty cashier gives employee amount spent │
│ out of petty cash box and puts voucher in │
│           petty cash box              │
└─────────────────────────────────────┘
                  ↓
┌─────────────────────────────────────┐
│ Voucher is recorded in petty cash book │
└─────────────────────────────────────┘
```

Petty cash box

- must be locked
- only petty cashier has access.

Imprest system

- most common system of controlling petty cash
- set amount of petty cash for period determined e.g. £100 per week
- cash paid out only when vouchers put into petty cash box
- at end of week petty cash box topped back up to £100 from bank account.

Monday	Friday	Friday
Petty cash box	Petty cash box	Petty cash box
£100 cash	£30 cash £70 vouchers	£100 (£70 withdrawn in cash from bank account. Vouchers removed and filed).

Non-imprest system

- another system of dealing with petty cash
- for example a set amount, say £100, being withdrawn in cash and put into the petty cash box each week no matter how much is paid out.

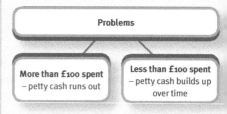

Problems

More than £100 spent – petty cash runs out

Less than £100 spent – petty cash builds up over time

Petty cash vouchers

- gives details of expenditure incurred by employee
- must normally be supported by receipt or other evidence of expense
- must include VAT for expense where VAT is reclaimable
- must be authorised before payment can be made.

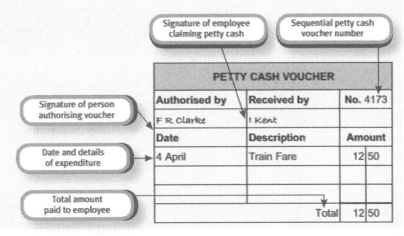

Signature of employee claiming petty cash

Sequential petty cash voucher number

Signature of person authorising voucher

Date and details of expenditure

Total amount paid to employee

PETTY CASH VOUCHER		
Authorised by	**Received by**	**No.** 4173
F R Clarke	I Kent	
Date	**Description**	**Amount**
4 April	Train Fare	12 50
	Total	12 50

Petty cash book

- book of prime entry
- often part of general ledger as well
- small cash receipts side
- larger analysed cash payments side.

PETTY CASH BOOK											
Receipts			Payments								
Date	Narrative	Total £	Date	Narrative	Voucher no	Total £	Postage £	Cleaning £	Tea & Coffee £	Sundry £	VAT £
1 Nov	Bal b/f	35.50									
1 Nov	Cheque	114.50	1 Nov	ASDA	58	23.50			23.50		
			2 Nov	Post Office Ltd	59	29.50	29.50				
			2 Nov	Cleaning materials	60	15.07		12.56			2.51
			3 Nov	Postage	61	16.19	16.19				
			3 Nov	ASDA	62	10.57		8.81			1.76
			4 Nov	Newspapers	63	18.90				18.90	
			5 Nov	ASDA	64	12.10				10.09	2.01
						125.83	45.69	21.37	23.50	28.99	6.28

Receipts side – only one column as only entry is regular payment in cash from bank

Payments side – analysed according to typical expenditure plus VAT column

Imprest amount of £150 to start week

Date of claim

Details

Sequential petty cash voucher numbers

Analysed payments – total column includes VAT but analysis column amount is net of VAT

When petty cash book has been written up for a period it must be totalled. Totals should then be checked by cross-casting:

	£
Postage	45.69
Cleaning	21.37
Tea & coffee	23.50
Sundry	28.99
VAT	6.28
Total	125.83

Topping up the petty cash box

- at the end of the period (in this case a week) the petty cash box will be topped up to the imprest amount
- this is done by taking cash out of the bank account
- amount is total of the petty cash expenditure – £125.83
- petty cash box should then have imprest amount of £150 in order to start following week.

Posting the petty cash book (PCB)

Petty cash book part of general ledger

- petty cash book is normally part of the general ledger.

Receipt of cash

- debit entry already in petty cash book
- only posting required is a credit in the cash payments book for the cash taken out of the bank (this should have been done from cheque stub anyway).

Petty cash payments

- credit entry in petty cash book (total column £125.83)
- debit entries required to each expense account and VAT account.

Example

Postage account		
	£	£
PCB	45.69	

Cleaning account		
	£	£
PCB	21.37	

Food and drink account		
	£	£
PCB	23.50	

Sundry expenses account		
	£	£
PCB	28.99	

VAT account		
	£	£
PCB	6.28	

Petty cash book not part of general ledger

- if the petty cash book is not part of the general ledger then a petty cash control account is required in the general ledger.

Petty cash receipt

- receipt of cash at start of week

  Debit Petty cash

  control account £114.50

  Credit Bank account £114.50

Petty cash payments

  Debit Postage £45.69

  Cleaning £21.37

  Food and drink £23.50

  Sundry expenses £28.99

  VAT £ 6.28

  Credit Petty cash

  control account £125.83

CBA focus

In the assessment you may have to write up or post the petty cash book to the general ledger accounts.

Reconciling petty cash

Under imprest system:

Therefore to check petty cash security:

- total cash in box
- total vouchers in box
- add together
- should equal imprest amount
- vouchers then removed from box, entered into petty cash book and filed.

Petty cash control account

If the petty cash book is not part of the general ledger there will be a petty cash control account in the general ledger which shows the summarised cash receipts and payments for the period.

Example

A petty cash system is run on an imprest system of £100. During the month of May petty cash expenditure totalled £68 and the petty cash box was topped back up to the imprest amount with a withdrawal of £68 cash from the bank.

Step 1 – Enter the imprest amount that would have been in the petty cash box at the start of the month – asset – debit balance.

Petty cash control account

	£		£
Opening balance	100		

Step 2 – Enter the total paid out in the month.

Petty cash control account

	£		£
Opening balance	100	Petty cash payments	68

Full double entry:

    Debit   Expense accounts

    Credit   Petty cash control account

Step 3 – Enter the cash paid into petty cash from the bank.

Petty cash control account

	£		£
Opening balance	100	Petty cash payments	68
Cash	68		

Full double entry:

    Debit   Petty cash control account

    Credit   Cash payments book

Step 4 – Carry down the balance at the end of the month – the imprest amount.

Petty cash control account

	£		£
Opening balance	100	Petty cash payments	68
Cash	68	Balance c/d	100
	168		168
Balance b/d	100		

Asset – debit balance

Topping up the petty cash box

- at the end of the period (in this case a week) the petty cash box will be topped up to the imprest amount
- this is done by taking cash out of the bank account
- amount is total of the petty cash expenditure – £68.00
- petty cash box should then have imprest amount of £100 in order to start following week.

Petty cash control account reconciliation

- at the end of a period the balance on the petty cash control account should equal the amount of cash in the petty cash box
- any difference must be investigated.

Differences

More cash than balance

- error in writing up petty cash book
- less cash given out than should have been

Less cash than balance

- error in writing up cash book
- too much cash out than should have been
- petty cash voucher omitted from petty cash book
- cash paid out without voucher
- cash could have been stolen

Index